KNOWING THE
ORISHA
GODS & GODDESSES

WALDETE TRISTÃO | ILLUSTRATED BY CACO BRESSANE

First English Edition, Third Printing, 2021

ISBN: 978-0-7387-6704-8

Llewellyn Publications
A Division of Llewellyn Worldwide Ltd. 2143 Wooddale Drive
Woodbury, MN 55125-2989 www.llewellyn.com

Printed in the United States of America

THANKS...

To Robson Gil, my beloved son, for always making me understand that my learning tasks are bigger than my teaching ones and for giving me the biggest challenge of life: to learn a new way every day to deal with your "present absence." Your absence is not and never will be unnoticed: you are and forever will be in my heart. To Gil—companion, love, and safe presence in my life; to Valquiria Tristão, my beloved sister; to Rodney, for saying, "go ahead and face the world, my daughter!"; to Roseane, friend of all hours; and to Diego, for motivating me to write again.

Waldete Tristão

To my beloved companion Florence, who beautifies my life every day, wherever I flower. To Surica and Paçoca, our little ones. To Puma, forever my most faithful squire. To my mother, Taïs, who teaches me the courage to face life; to dear Aviro and my sister Alice. To my grandmother Zita, forever my inspiration. To always wonderful Cris Blue. To my father, Antonio José Lopes, Professor Mustache, for his passion for teaching. To Rodney, for the good luck of the good dates.

Caco Bressane

ONCE UPON A TIME...

Did you know that every stone, every little plant, every breeze, and every ray of sunshine has the power of the Orishas within? Yeah! The Orishas are African gods: forces of nature that guide us and protect us for life. Many, many years ago, they were brought across the ocean to the Americas by enslaved Africans.

When the world was created by the Orishas, there was no separation between Orun, the heaven, and Aiyê, the earth. Human beings and Orishas were able to come and go between heaven and earth, playing, dancing, and sharing their lives and their adventures with each other. They ate and drank together, hunted, planted, harvested, experienced love and sadness, and also knew how to do very special things!

Our elders say that Orun's sacred space was very close to Aiyê, but one day one of the human beings touched their muddy hands in the sacred white of Orun, and Olodumare, the supreme god, became very angry! They say that he blew and snorted, separating heaven and earth forever...

The Orishas missed their adventures with humans and were very saddened by this separation, so they decided to ask Olodumare for the ability to return to earth from time to time to visit their friends. The supreme god, seeing the sadness in the eyes of the Orishas, allowed it, and this is how it has been since the creation of the world!

From all these adventures, amazing stories have sprung up. The Orishas have so much to tell us, and we have so much to learn! Let's get to know a little more about each of them.

ESHU

ESHU IS ALWAYS THE FIRST ORISHA AND COMES DRESSED IN RED AND BLACK, BUT HE ALSO LIKES TO MIX ALL THE COLORS IN THE WORLD. HE HAS MANY NAMES AND NICKNAMES; IN SOME PARTS OF BRAZIL, HE'S ALSO CALLED BARÁ. HE IS THE MESSENGER BETWEEN HUMANS AND THE ORISHAS AND THE KEEPER OF THE CROSSROADS AND THE FRONT DOOR. HE'S ALSO THE ONE WHO OPENS THE WAY FOR US WHEN TIMES ARE TOUGH. HIS SYMBOLS ARE THE OGÓ (A KIND OF WOODEN STICK WITH ONE ROUNDED TIP) AND SEVERAL KEYS.

ESHU IS ALSO THE ONE WHO TAKES ALL OUR REQUESTS, PROMISES, AND THANKS AND DELIVERS THEM TO OTHER ORISHAS—AND THAT'S WHY WE SAY THAT ESHU IS OUR BEST FRIEND, BECAUSE HE CARES FOR US WHEN WE ARE AROUND! HE EATS EVERYTHING, BUT HIS PREFERENCE IS GOAT AND ROOSTER MEAT, CRUMBS WITH PALM OIL, AND A SIDE OF CACHAÇA. ESHU'S DAY IS MONDAY, AND TO HONOR HIM, WE SAY ALOUD, "LAROIÊ," WHICH MEANS "HAIL THE OWNER OF ALL POWER." AND YOU—WHAT'S YOUR FAVORITE DAY OF THE WEEK?

OGUN

HERE COMES ESHU'S INSEPARABLE BROTHER, THE HAUGHTY WARRIOR IN NAVY BLUE: OGUN, THE ORISHA OF BATTLES, IRON, AND TECHNOLOGY. THEY ARE SO INSEPARABLE THAT THEY EVEN WORK TOGETHER. AS ESHU IS THE ONE WHO OPENS THE WAY, OGUN IS THE ONE WHO TAKES CARE OF THE SAFETY OF TRAVELERS ON THE ROADS. OGUN IS ALSO RESPONSIBLE FOR THE PROGRESS OF LIFE, ALWAYS GOING STRONG AND WIELDING HIS OBÉ, A TYPE OF MACHETE THAT HE USES TO BREAK THROUGH AND OVERCOME ALL OF LIFE'S OBSTACLES.

OGUN'S DAY IS TUESDAY. TO HONOR THIS GREAT WARRIOR, WE SAY, "OGUN IYE," WHICH MEANS "OGUN, I RESPECT YOU!" HE IS VERY FOND OF EATING ROOSTER AND GOAT MEAT, ALONG WITH ROASTED YAM AND PALM OIL, BUT HIS FAVORITE DISH IS A GOOD FEIJOADA! AND YOU—WHAT IS YOUR FAVORITE FOOD?

OSHOSI

THIS IS OSHOSI, THE KING OF KETU. HE IS GOD OF ABUNDANCE, PROSPERITY, AND HAPPINESS. OSHOSI LIVES ON THE BANKS OF RIVERS AND IN THE MIDDLE OF FORESTS, AND HIS CLOTHES ARE TURQUOISE OR LIGHT GREEN. IN ONE HAND HE CARRIES THE ERUQUERE (A BEE SCARECROW MADE WITH A HORSE'S MANE, WHICH SYMBOLIZES HIS ROYALTY) AND IN THE OTHER, THE BOW AND ARROW, WITH WHICH HE HUNTS AND EARNS A LIVING. OSHOSI'S DANCE SHOWCASES A HUNTING SCENE, FROM THE CHASE TO THE MOMENT HE SHOOTS THE ARROW AND HITS HIS TARGET! HAVE YOU EVER PLAYED BOW AND ARROW LIKE A HUNTER?

OSHOSI LIKES TO EAT ALL KINDS OF MEATS, SUCH AS TIGER, ELEPHANT, OX, AND GOAT, AS IN A LARGE BARBECUE! HE ALSO LOVES DISHES PREPARED WITH CORN AND COCONUT, ESPECIALLY AXOXO, WHICH IS PREPARED WITH BOILED CORN, WHITE WINE, A PINCH OF SALT, AND COCONUT CHIPS FOR GARNISH. OSHOSI'S DAY IS THURSDAY, AND WE GREET OSHOSI BY SAYING, "OKE ARO, AROLE," WHICH MEANS "SAVE THE GREAT HUNTER."

OMOLU

THAT STRAW COVER IS OMOLU, ALSO CALLED OBALUAIE: "KING OF THE EARTH GROUND," GOD OF HEALTH AND LIFE! OMOLU KNOWS ALL KINDS OF DISEASES, AND, BEST OF ALL, HE KNOWS THEIR CURES AND SPREADS THEM AROUND THE WORLD! THAT'S WHY WE MAKE OFFERINGS AND PRAYERS TO OMOLU WHEN SOMEONE IS SICK. OMOLU DANCES LIKE AN OLD MAN, STARING AT THE GROUND, SHAKING HIS BODY AS IF HAVING DIFFICULTY BALANCING, AND ALWAYS CARRYING HIS RED, BLACK, AND WHITE SHELL NECKLACES WITH HIM.

IN HIS HAND, HE BEARS HIS SHASHARA, A TYPE OF STRAW BROOM MADE OF DRIED PALM LEAVES, WHICH HE USES TO WARD OFF DISEASE. OMOLU'S FAVORITE DAY IS MONDAY, AS IS OUR FRIEND ESHU'S. WE SALUTE HIM BY SAYING, "ATOTO," THAT IS, "SILENCE! THE KING HAS COME." OMOLU LIKES TO EAT GOAT, PORK, AND ROOSTER MEAT, BUT GUESS WHAT? WHAT HE LIKES MOST IS POPCORN GARNISHED WITH COCONUT STRIPS, WHICH IS CALLED DEBURU! HAVE YOU EVER EATEN POPCORN WITH COCONUT? WHY NOT TRY IT OUT?

OSSAIN

THIS IS OSSAIN, THE GREAT SCIENTIST OF THE ORISHAS! CARRYING AN IRON BIRD IN HIS HANDS AND MANY GOURDS AROUND HIS WAIST, HE COMES DRESSED IN GREEN AND WHITE, DANCING ON ONE LEG; HE EVEN SEEMS TO BE PICKING LEAVES ON THE GROUND. OSSAIN LIVES IN THE MIDDLE OF THE FOREST AND HIGH IN THE TREES, WHERE HE SPENDS HIS DAYS STUDYING AND DISCOVERING THE MYSTERIES OF ALL PLANTS AND THE POWERS OF LEAVES AND HERBS. WITH THEM, HE PREPARES ALL THE MEDICINES IN THE WORLD.

BY THE WAY, HAS ANYONE IN YOUR FAMILY EVER PREPARED A TEA FOR YOU TO GET BETTER FROM THE FLU? SO YOU HAVE ALREADY PROVED THE POWERS OF THIS GREAT ORISHA! OSSAIN LIKES TO EAT GOAT MEAT AND ROOSTERS, BUT HIS FAVORITE FEAST IS BOILED CORN, VEGETABLES, AND FRUITS OF ALL KINDS. OSSAIN'S DAY IS THURSDAY, AND TO ASK FOR HIS PROTECTION, WE SAY, "EUE ASSA," WHICH MEANS "WE HONOR THE POWER OF THE LEAVES."

OSHUMARE

OSHUMARE IS GOD OF TRANSFORMATIONS, OF ALL THINGS THAT END AND BEGIN, AND OF INFINITY. LIKE HIS FRIENDS OSHOSI, OMOLU, AND SHANGO (WHOM YOU'LL SOON MEET), OSHUMARE IS ALSO AN AFRICAN KING, AND IN THE COUNTRIES WHERE HE REIGNS, HE IS REPRESENTED AS A SERPENT: THE SYMBOL OF WISDOM. HIS CLOTHES ARE YELLOW, GREEN, AND BLACK, LIKE THE SKIN OF SNAKES. WHEN OSHUMARE DANCES, HE MOVES POINTING UP AND DOWN, SHOWING THAT HEAVEN AND EARTH ARE CONNECTED.

OSHUMARE'S DAY, TOGETHER WITH OGUN, IS TUESDAY, AND WE GREET HIM BY SAYING, "AHOBOBOI," THE GREATEST HONOR FOR THIS KING'S SUBJECTS! AS THE LORD OF INFINITY, OSHUMARE IS ALSO THE GOD OF ALL LONG THINGS, THE CONTINUATION OF LIFE, AND VISION. HE LIKES TO EAT GOAT AND DRAKE, A TYPE OF WILD DUCK, AND ALSO LOVES A SWEET POTATO MASH! HAVE YOU EVER EATEN SWEET POTATOES? THEY'RE DELICIOUS!

NANA

This lady sitting here is Nana, mother of all creation. She is goddess of still waters, mud that lies at the bottom of lakes, and clay. Nana uses a curtain of shells to cover her face and wears white, blue, and lilac. She is goddess of thoughts and has wisdom as her soul mate, being the oldest of all the orishas and mother of Omolu, Oshumare, and Ossain.

Nana dances slowly and carries with her the ibiri (a staff made with the stalks of palm leaves) as if it were a child in her arms. Sometimes when she dances, she makes slight movements with her hands, seemingly grinding boiled and peeled beans, her favorite food. Nana also likes to eat goat meat accompanied by aberém, a dumpling made with white cornmeal, and omi toro, a very sweet porridge. Have you ever eaten porridge like this? The day of Nana is Saturday, and to honor this great elder, we say, "Saluba," which means "save the mother of all mothers."

OSHUN

OSHUN IS THE GODDESS WHO LIVES IN FRESH WATER, RIVERS, STREAMS, AND WATERFALLS. SHE IS THE ORISHA OF GOLD, FERTILITY, AND LOVE. DRESSED BEAUTIFULLY IN YELLOW AND GOLD, OSHUN IS ALSO THE PROTECTOR OF CHILDREN AND PREGNANCY. HER DANCE IS LIKE A FISH IN WATER, AND SHE LOVINGLY COMBS HER HAIR WHILE WEARING HER EARRINGS, BRACELETS, AND NECKLACES. DO YOU ALSO LIKE TO SPRUCE YOURSELF UP? WHAT'S YOUR FAVORITE ACCESSORY?

OSHUN'S SYMBOL IS THE ABEBE, A FAN-SHAPED MIRROR IN WHICH SHE ADMIRES HER OWN BEAUTY. OSHUN LIKES TO EAT GOAT AND CHICKEN MEAT, BUT HER FAVORITE DISH IS OMOLOCUM, A RECIPE MADE WITH BOILED FRENCH BEANS, DRIED SHRIMP, AND BOILED EGGS. SATURDAY IS HER SPECIAL DAY, AND THE GREETING TO OSHUN IS "ORE IEIE O," WHICH IS THE SAME AS SAYING, "SAVE THE LADY OF ALL BEAUTY AND SWEETNESS."

IBEYI

HOW CUTE ARE THESE TWO CHILDREN: THE TWINS IBEYI, ORISHAS OF CHILDHOOD AND INNOCENCE! A BOY AND A GIRL BORN AT THE SAME TIME AND ALWAYS PLAYING TOGETHER, THEY TEACH US THAT THOSE WHO ARE DIFFERENT ARE MUCH MORE SIMILAR TO US THAN WE THINK. THE TWINS ARE RELATED TO EVERYTHING THAT BEGINS: THE SOURCE OF A RIVER, THE BIRTH OF HUMAN BEINGS, THE GERMINATION OF PLANTS, AND SO ON. IBEYI WEAR LIGHT BLUE AND PINK, BUT THEY LIKE ALL COLORS AND LOVE PRANKS.

IBEYI REPRESENT THE JOY, INNOCENCE, AND PURITY OF ALL CHILDREN, AND THEY ARE THE ONES WHO PROTECT BABIES FROM BIRTH TO ADOLESCENCE. HAVE YOU EVER SEEN A NEWBORN BABY? SO CUTE! THE TWINS' FAVORITE FOOD IS CALLED CARURU, A DELIGHT MADE WITH COOKED OKRA, BUT, LIKE CHILDREN, THEY ALSO LOVE ALL KINDS OF SWEETS. THEY JUMP WITH JOY WHEN WE SAY TO THEM, "EGBE! IBEYI ERO," MEANING "HEY TWINS, LET'S ALL PLAY TOGETHER!"

OBBA

LOOK WHO'S COMING NOW, DRESSED IN ORANGE AND BROWN—IT'S OBBA, THE MOST PASSIONATE AND BRAVE OF ALL THE ORISHAS! SHE IS THE OLDEST WIFE OF SHANGO, BUT, BEING VERY ANGRY, SHE LIVES ALONE. PROTECTOR OF HOME AND FAMILIES, SHE CAN BECOME A LIONESS WHEN NEEDED TO DEFEND THE PEOPLE SHE LOVES. IS THERE SOMEONE IN YOUR FAMILY LIKE OBBA WHO PROTECTS YOU AND THE PEOPLE YOU LOVE?

DURING HER DANCE, OBBA HOLDS HER SWORD AND SHIELD AND COVERS HER HEAD WITH A BEAUTIFUL TURBAN SO THAT NO ONE REALIZES SHE LOST AN EAR DURING A BATTLE. SHE ALSO CARRIES AN ARROW LIKE OSHOSI, SHOWING THAT SHE'S A HUNTER IN ADDITION TO A WARRIOR. OBBA LIKES GOAT MEAT AND CHICKEN, BUT HER FAVORITE FOOD IS ABARÁ, A FRENCH BEAN CAKE COOKED WITH SHRIMP AND PALM OIL. HER GREETING IS "OBA SHIRE," WHICH MEANS "HAIL THE LADY WARRIOR," AND HER DAY OF THE WEEK IS WEDNESDAY, AS IS SHANGO'S, OSHUN'S, AND OYÁ'S.

IYEWA

IYEWA IS THE FEMALE VERSION OF OSHUMARE; SHE'S GODDESS OF FOUNTAINS, BEAUTY, VISION, AND ALL THAT IS MYSTERIOUS AND HIDDEN. SHE ALSO REPRESENTS PURITY AND INNOCENCE AND YOUTH, AND SHE ESPECIALLY PROTECTS YOUNGER GIRLS AND ADOLESCENTS. WHEN IYEWA DANCES, SHE MOVES HER WHOLE BODY LIKE AN ENCHANTED SERPENT, HOLDING AN IRON SNAKE IN ONE HAND AND CARRYING HER ADOBE, A GOURD IN WHICH SHE KEEPS HER SECRETS. DO YOU ALSO HAVE ENCHANTED SECRETS LIKE HER?

HER FAVORITE COLORS ARE RED, PINK, AND TERRACOTTA, A TYPE OF BROWN. SHE IS VERY FOND OF EATING GOAT MEAT, BLACK BEANS WITH BOILED EGGS, AND PLANTAINS FRIED IN PALM OIL, BUT HER FAVORITE FOOD IS CALLED DANBORO: A BLEND OF ALL HER FAVORITE INGREDIENTS COOKED AND FRIED. THE DAY OF THE WEEK THAT IYEWA LIKES MOST IS SATURDAY, AND WE GREET THIS BEAUTIFUL ORISHA BY SAYING LOUDLY, "HIHÓ."

27

OYÁ

OYÁ, ALSO CALLED YANSAN, COMES AS A STORM; SHE IS GODDESS OF WINDS AND STORMS. A STRONG AND INDEPENDENT WOMAN, SHE IS SHANGO'S WIFE AND ACCOMPANIES HIM IN DAILY BATTLES. SHE IS THE MOTHER OF NINE CHILDREN: SOME OF THEM SHE GAVE BIRTH TO, AND THE OTHERS SHE ADOPTED, RAISED, AND LOVED! OYÁ LIVES AMONG THE BAMBOO GROVES, AND SHE PROTECTS HUMANS FROM THE FURY OF LIGHTNING. HAVE YOU EVER HEARD THE WIND SING ON RAINY DAYS? IT IS OYÁ COMING TO PROTECT US!

SHE IS DRESSED IN BROWN, RED, PINK, OR WHITE, AND HER DANCE RESEMBLES THE RAGING WINDS. WIELDING HER SWORD AND ERUESHIM, A KIND OF BUFFALO-HAIR DUSTER, SHE MOVES AS A WARRIOR IN COMBAT. OYÁ LIKES GOAT AND CHICKEN MEAT, BUT SHE PREFERS A GOOD ACARAJÉ, A FRIED DUMPLING MADE WITH FRENCH BEANS. JUST LIKE SHANGO, OYÁ'S FAVORITE DAY IS WEDNESDAY, AND WE GREET HER BY SAYING, "EPAHEI OYÁ," WHICH MEANS "SAVE THE MAJESTIC WINDS OF OYÁ."

LOGUNEDÉ

DRESSED IN BLUE AND YELLOW, LOGUNEDÉ WALKS LIKE A SLENDER PEACOCK, PROUD OF HIS BEAUTY. HAVE YOU EVER SEEN A PEACOCK WITH ITS TAIL OPEN? REMEMBER ITS COLORS? THIS IS LOGUNEDÉ, THE PRINCE OF ORISHAS, GOD OF HUNTING AND FISHING! SON OF OSHOSI AND OSHUN, HE LIVES SIX MONTHS IN THE WOODS WITH HIS FATHER AND SIX MONTHS IN THE RIVERS WITH HIS MOTHER.

HE IS THE CHILD GOD WHOM THE ELDERS RESPECT—THE LORD OF JOY AND WEALTH! HE BEARS IN HIS HANDS THE BOW AND ARROW THAT HE RECEIVED FROM HIS FATHER AND THE ABEBE, THE MIRROR-FAN HE RECEIVED FROM HIS MOTHER. LOGUNEDÉ ALSO SHARES THE TASTES OF HIS PARENTS, SO HE LIKES TO EAT GOAT MEAT, ROOSTER AND CHICKEN, FRUITS, AND A DISH MADE HALF WITH OSHOSI'S AXOXO AND THE OTHER HALF WITH OSHUN'S OMOLOCUM. HIS DAY OF THE WEEK IS THURSDAY, AND HE IS VERY HAPPY WHEN WE TELL HIM, "LOCI LOCI! ELU ARO!"

YEMAYA

This is Yemaya, the great mother who cares for all of us, humans and orishas; she is the goddess of the sea and motherhood. Yemaya teaches us that respecting the opinions of others does not mean agreeing with them and also teaches us to forgive. Her clothes are sky blue or very light green and white, like the waters and the foam on the waves of the sea. In her hands she holds an abebe, like Oshun, but hers is made of silver and is shaped like fish.

Yemaya dances by waving her hands as if carrying water to cleanse the whole world and wash evil away. Have you seen how the waves come and go on the shore? Such is the dance of Yemaya. She likes to eat sheep, paws, fish meat, rice, and also shrimp-spiced hominy (ebo iya), her favorite dish. Yemaya's day is Saturday, and we greet her by saying, "Odo iya," which means "save the mother of the waters."

33

SHANGO

THIS ONE IS SHANGO, THE MIGHTY KING OF OYÓ, AN OLD KING-
DOM IN ANCIENT AFRICA. GOD OF VOLCANOES, LIGHTNING, AND
THUNDER, HE IS ONE OF THE MOST WELL-KNOWN ORISHAS. HAVE
YOU EVER HEARD THUNDER ON STORMY DAYS? THUNDER IS THE
VOICE OF SHANGO, GOD OF JUSTICE AND TRUTH. THE SCALE IS
ONE OF HIS SYMBOLS; HE WEIGHS THE MISTAKES AND SUCCESSES
OF OUR LIVES! WHILE LIVING AMONG HUMANS, HE WAS MARRIED
TO THE ORISHAS OBBA, THE BRAVE WARRIOR; OYÁ, THE INDEPEN-
DENT; AND OSHUN, THE BEAUTIFUL.

HOLDING HIS OXE, A TWO-BLADED AXE, AND DRESSED IN LONG
STRIPS OF RED, BROWN, OR WHITE CLOTH, SHANGO DANCES JOY-
FULLY, TELLING THE STORY OF HIS LIFE AND KINGDOM. HE LIKES
TO EAT EVERYTHING AND LOVES MUTTON AND ROOSTER, BUT HIS
FAVORITE FOOD IS CALLED AMALÁ, A DISH MADE FROM COOKED
OKRA. HIS DAY IS WEDNESDAY, AND TO HONOR HIM, WE SAY, "KAO
KABIESILE," WHICH MEANS "GIVE US PERMISSION TO LOOK AT THE
KING."

OSHALA

THIS GENTLEMAN, LOOKING LIKE A TIRED OLD MAN, IS OSHALA. HE ALWAYS WEARS WHITE TO SYMBOLIZE HIS NAME, WHICH MEANS "THE LORD OF THE WHITE CLOTHS," AND HE IS SOMETIMES ALSO CALLED OSHALUFAN OR OBATALA. HE KNOWS THE SECRETS OF LIFE AND DEATH AND IS THEREFORE HIGHLY RESPECTED BY ALL OTHER ORISHAS. HE IS THE GOD OF CREATION, THE ONE WHO SHAPED HUMANS FROM THE CLAY OF NANA.

OSHALA MOVES SLOWLY AND CARRIES IN HIS HANDS THE OPASHORO, A STAFF ON WHICH HE RESTS AS IF IT WERE A CANE. AT THE SLIGHTEST TOUCH OF THAT STAFF ON THE GROUND, OSHALA INVITES ALL THE OTHER ORISHAS TO COME TO EARTH AND DANCE WITH HIM. DO YOU KNOW AN OLDER PERSON WHO ALSO USES A CANE? THESE PEOPLE ARE OFTEN WISE AND HAVE A LOT TO TEACH US! OSHALA LIKES TO EAT SNAILS AND WHITE FOODS, SO HIS FAVORITE FOOD IS THE EBO, THE WHITE CORN COOKED WITHOUT ANY SPICE OR SALT. OSHALA'S DAY IS FRIDAY, AND ON THAT DAY, WE SHOULD ALL WEAR WHITE IN HIS HONOR. THE GREETING OF THIS GREAT ORISHA IS "EPA BABA," WHICH MEANS "OH ADMIRABLE FATHER."

OSHOGUIAN

THIS BRAVE BOY IS OSHOGUIAN, THE WARRIOR OF PEACE WHO DEFENDS US AND SOLVES ALL PROBLEMS IN OUR LIVES! HE IS RELATED TO OSHALA AND THEREFORE DRESSES ALL IN WHITE, WEARING ONLY A FEW LIGHT BLUE DETAILS ON HIS NECKLACES. HE IS GOD OF CULTURE, PROGRESS, AND WORK, AND HE ENSURES THE LIVELIHOOD OF FAMILIES. HE EVEN INVENTED THE PESTLE, THE FIRST TOOL USED TO PREPARE FOOD.

OSHOGUIAN DANCES STEADILY AND PROUDLY, HOLDING IN ONE HAND A SWORD AND IN THE OTHER A PYLON, BOTH SILVER-MADE. HAVE YOU EVER HAD A SWORD BATTLE WITH A FRIEND AND MADE PEACE IN THE END? JUST LIKE YOU AND YOUR FRIEND, OSHOGUIAN SOMETIMES CARRIES A WHITE FLAG ON HIS BACK TO SYMBOLIZE THE PEACE HE IS SEEKING FOR US! OSHOGUIAN LIKES TO EAT SNAILS, MASHED YAMS WITH OLIVE OIL, RICE, AND HOMINY—ALL WITHOUT SALT AND WITHOUT SPICES. LIKE OSHALA, HIS DAY OF THE WEEK IS FRIDAY, AND THE GREETING IN HIS HONOR IS "EPA BABA!"

ABOUT THE AUTHORS

WALDETE TRISTÃO

I love to listen to and tell stories, and I did this for a long time as a kindergarten teacher, academic coordinator, and trainer in basic education. I think of stories as powerful tools to shape people. In the area of education, I hold a PhD from the University of São Paulo and a master's degree from the Pontifical Catholic University of São Paulo. I work as a consultant for the Center for Studies on Labor Relations and Inequalities in projects related to ethnic-racial relations and childhood. I also participate in Ilu Oba de Min, an educational and Black art cultural group.

CACO BRESSANE

I am an illustrator. I graduated with a degree in architecture and urbanism from Escola da Cidade in São Paulo in 2007 and mastered in urbanism from PROURB-UFRJ in Rio de Janeiro in 2010. As an architect, I was part of an office team until 2012. After that, I pursued my dream of drawing and worked for almost four years at Kiwi Studio. I currently run my own graphic design and illustration studio. I have illustrated for major publishers and for many different genres, including children's books, as well as newspapers and magazines.

This book was originally published in the spring of 2018 in the city of São Paulo for the memory and resistance of all African and African-descendant people.